The Bible Savvy Believer

Dr. Jerry Gibson
Kathy Johns

All Scripture in this book is from the New American Standard Bible (NASB) unless otherwise identified as (NCV) from the New Century Version or (NIV) from the New International Version of the Bible. Please note that all Scripture is punctuated exactly as each Bible version requires. The New American Standard Bible capitalizes pronouns referring to God, while the other versions do not. The NASB also uses all small capital letters in New Testament verses that refer to verses in the Old Testament.

ISBN 978-1-935298-10-6

Truth Book Publishers
Franklin, Illinois
www.truthbookpublishers.com

DEDICATIONS

This book is dedicated to my devoted and faithful wife, Normadeene, our four children, Albert Joseph, Cynthia Charlotte, Gerald Arthur, Jr., and Rebecca Joan, our five granddaughters, Emily Gibson, Anna Gibson Lee, Melissa Vale Gacina, and Laura and Carly Henriksen, and our great-grandchildren, Isabella Gibson and Noah Lee. Also to the thousands of young men and women who have allowed us to be their mentors, and their parents for allowing us to do so.

Jerry Gibson

To Ken, Greg, and Steve Johns, the beloved family the Lord gave me, and to my dear dad, Neil Mehler.

Kathy Johns

To our graphic artists, Ben and Tanya Mueller, for their cover design.

To our friend and editor, Laura Fox Distler.

CONTENTS

CHAPTER I

More Like Him

We can easily list tangible reasons why we chose our occupations, our homes, our cars, our friends, or our spouses. But, can we easily explain why we chose Jesus Christ as our Savior? What words follow our "because" when we are asked why we believe? What Scripture, even if it was only one verse, led us to trust in Jesus?

As Christians, we need to know what the Bible says in order to understand and articulate in whom, what, and why we believe. We must be ever-ready to answer the same question Pontius Pilate posed 2,000 years ago: "'Then what shall I do with Jesus who is called Christ?'" Matthew 27:22. That is the most important question we will ever be asked and we need to have a compelling answer.

We are too often better-educated consumers, voters, and sports fans than we are Christians, having read more about products, candidates, and athletes than our Lord and Savior. We need to be as conscientious about educating ourselves about God by reading His manual, His resume, and His statistics.

Just as "Romeo and Juliet" is required reading for high school students, the Bible should be required reading for Christians. If we haven't read the book, then we won't succeed on the book report, which in Christian terms is what we think, say, and do. In other words, we *will* be tested on this material by how we live our lives. It is simply not enough to hear a homily, sermon, or Scripture reading at church and then ignore the Bible for the rest of the week. The weekly service is supposed to inspire us, not just satisfy us, for a week of Christian growth and service. We need to fortify that weekly message by reading the Bible.

There is no better role model than Jesus Christ and biblical knowledge is essential in knowing who He is and how we should behave as His followers. Biographies of great people often top our reading lists and Jesus certainly has no rival in that category. The Bible is the Lord's biography; it is His gracious revelation of who He is and just how much He loves us. Scripture is the very mind of God revealed to man. He has all the facts because He created all the facts. "How precious to me are your thoughts, O God! How vast is the sum of them!" Psalm 139:17 (NIV). "Oh, the depth of the riches both of the wisdom and knowledge of God! How unsearchable are His judgments and unfathomable His ways!" Romans 11:33. What an opportunity God has given us to know Him!

When we know what the Bible says, we can more confidently and accurately answer that all-important question—what would Jesus do? That is the question we should ask ourselves before making any important decisions. He needs to be the Lord in *all* aspects of our lives, not just in those areas that we pick and choose. Following Jesus is not a hobby. God is not God occasionally so we don't want to be just occasional followers. He does not sleep, vacation, or ignore us. "'My Father never stops working, and so I keep working, too,'" Jesus says in John 5:17 (NCV). He is always with us and we need to remember that when we decide what to do with our time. Are we going someplace He would want us to go? Would we feel comfortable taking Him there with us? Are we doing something Jesus would want us to do? When we become Christians, our life is no longer divided between the secular and the sacred; it all becomes holy.

When we acknowledge Jesus as our Lord and Savior, we must make Him our highest priority. If we were playing football, basketball, baseball, or soccer, our coach would advise us to "keep our eyes on the ball" or even "be the ball" metaphorically. Our focus must be on the ball in order to succeed. And so it is with our Christian life; Jesus needs to be the center of our attention. "He is also head of the body, the church; and He is the beginning, the firstborn from the dead, so that He Himself will come to have first place in everything." Colossians 1:18.

That is a hard task for all of us. All too often we preach better than we live. Instead, we need to honor what we profess by what we practice. We cannot have the Lord's Supper and the Devil's dessert. Rather, we are to present our bodies as "a living and holy sacrifice, acceptable to God," according to Romans 12:1. In other words, we should put our whole selves in—not just an arm or a leg—and fully live our faith from head to toe and moment to moment. Sadly, our human imperfection constantly interferes with our ability to be worthy living sacrifices to God and we end up rolling right off the altar.

Very few people read the four Gospels. They read the fifth Gospel—our lives. Perhaps the greatest way to confess our faith in Christ is by the life we live. This poem emphasizes that point:

You are writing a Gospel a chapter a day,
By the deeds that you do and the words that you say.
Man reads what you write, whether faithless or true.
Say, what is the Gospel according to you?

It is frustrating when those who claim to be Christians do not practice the simple, basic principles Jesus teaches us in the New Testament. Philippians 1:27 tells us that we are to conduct ourselves "in a manner worthy of the gospel of Christ." As children of God, we are to be "above reproach" and "lights in the world," Philippians 2:15 says. Scripture must never be manipulated to fit our lifestyles. Rather, our lifestyles must be transformed to reflect Scripture.

The word "Christian" is the name "Christ" with the Latin suffix "ian," which means characteristic of, belonging or relating to, like or resembling. A Christian, by that definition, is supposed to be someone who has the nature of Christ. "Therefore if anyone is in Christ, *he is* a new creature; the old things passed away; behold, new things have come." II Corinthians 5:17.

True Christians are truly repentant and want to conform to Christ's standards. Repentance results in a change in our thinking, which leads to a change in our feelings, which then leads to a change in our actions. It involves a complete turn-around in the direction of our lives. Repentance works two ways: it first turns men God-ward and then it turns God man-ward. Any repentance too weak to be seen is not true scriptural repentance. "You were taught to leave your old self—to stop living the evil way you lived before. That old self becomes worse, because people are fooled by the evil things they want to do. But you were taught to be made new in your hearts, to become a new person. That new person is made to be like God—made to be truly good and holy." Ephesians 4:22-24 (NCV).

The story of the Prodigal (meaning recklessly wasteful) Son in Luke 15:11-32 is an excellent example of this. A young man asks his father for an early inheritance and with it, leaves home to squander it all on wild living. Humbled and enlightened by his mistakes, he returns home with a genuine change of heart seeking his father's forgiveness and mercy. His father is elated and celebrates that his once lost son is now found. In the same way, our repentance and petition for God's forgiveness should boldly show as we walk in a newness of life.

Unfortunately, most people see only the abuse of Christianity and not the real thing. Consider the dutiful churchgoer who is stingily kind, happy, thankful, fair, or cooperative; that's rather confusing "Christian" behavior. We are woefully imperfect messengers for a perfect God. Thankfully, it is never too late to become better messengers. We can do that by being more receptive to God, doing what He asks us to do, trusting that He truly is who He says He is, and striving to become more like Him. That is powerful living!

Firstly, we must aim to know God better, love Him more, and have full faith and reliance on Him. Again, that comes from reading the Bible and learning about who He is. Our best relationships are with those with whom we best communicate. Mutual understanding, acceptance, trust, and respect produce strong, honest, deep, and enduring friendships. We want people to "get" us just as they want us to "get" them. Reciprocity is an essential part of any substantive and progressive friendship. Our relationship with God should be no different. He certainly knows who we are; we should certainly know who He is. The inevitable outcome of knowing God better through Scripture is an increase in our love and trust in Him.

Secondly, we must love and trust God so much that we are satisfied despite our circumstances. An extreme example of this can be found in the book of Job, where the title character's fervent dedication to God surpassed his unimaginable suffering. The Lord allowed the Devil to profoundly test Job, who is described in Job 1:8 as "a blameless and upright man" who feared God and turned away from evil. He had 10 children, and his great material wealth included much livestock and many servants. The Devil's abuse starts in Job 1:13 with the loss of Job's livestock, his servants, and ultimately his precious children. But he continues to worship God by saying, "'The LORD gave and the LORD has taken away. Blessed be the name of the LORD.′ Through all this Job did not sin nor did he blame God." Job 1:21-22.

Thirdly, we must love our fellow man enough not to envy his or her situation. The Tenth Commandment is very clear on this: "'You shall not covet your neighbor's house; you shall not covet your neighbor's wife or his male servant or his female servant or his ox or his donkey or anything that belongs to your neighbor.′" Exodus 20:17. Instead, we are to be "devoted to one another in brotherly love," as Romans 12:10 tells us. The Bible tells us in detail just exactly what our brotherly Christian love should look like: "Love is patient, love is kind *and* is not jealous; love does not brag *and* is not arrogant, does not act unbecomingly; it does not seek its own, is not provoked, does not take into account a wrong *suffered,* does not rejoice in unrighteousness, but rejoices with the truth." I Corinthians 13:4-6. "'By this all men will know that you are My disciples, if you have love for one another.′" John 13:35.

CHAPTER II

Read All About Him

The Bible should serve as the compass that guides us in everything that we say and do. It should be the guidepost for our moral standards. Our tremendous freedom of choice can also offer us tremendous temptation, and conflicting opinions as to what is right and what is wrong. We will get a variety of advice throughout our lives, but the word of God *never* changes. It should be our absolute authority. "'Heaven and earth will pass away, but My words will not pass away,'" Jesus tells us in Matthew 24:35, Mark 13:31, and Luke 21:33. "The grass withers, the flower fades, but the word of our God stands forever." Isaiah 40:8.

The biblically savvy are not easily swayed by bad advice posing as wisdom. Scripturc tells us what is genuine; when we know what is true, we can determine what is false. We might not realize just how bad a stale cup of coffee tastes until we have enjoyed the fresh taste of a cup made from newly ground beans. Peter warns us in II Peter 2:1-3 that false teachers will malign the truth, exploit us with lies, introduce "destructive heresies," and even deny God. But, if we are Bible-smart, we will recognize the counterfeit.

"For the word of the LORD is right and true; he is faithful in all he does." Psalm 33:4 (NIV).

"Remember the LORD in all you do, and he will give you success. Don't depend on your own wisdom. Respect the LORD and refuse to do wrong," Proverbs 3:6-7 (NCV) counsels. The Creator of the universe wants to mentor us. Let's take Him up on His offer by making Scripture our daily advice column. "The LORD says, `I will make you wise and show you where to go. I will guide you and watch over you.'" Psalm 32:8 (NCV). We need only pick up our Bibles for that godly direction.

Once there was a great pastor who answered every question posed to him with the very same response. No matter what the question or concern, no matter who the asker, he would say, "Let's look at *The Book*, shall we?" He found no better advice or comfort than God's unwavering, perfect word.

Jesus didn't respond to those who questioned Him with "I think" or "I believe," but was quick to refer to what God tells us in the Scriptures. We need to be able to do the same. We need to provide book, chapter, and verse for the answers we give. Jesus asks God in John 17:17 to teach and purify us with the truth of His word.

Paul, the most prolific New Testament writer, confirms that the Bible is God's holy word in Galatians 1:11-12 when he says: "For I would have you know, brethren, that the gospel which was preached by me is not according to man. For I neither received it from man, nor was I taught it, but *I received it* through a revelation of Jesus Christ." Those are critical words. We are not followers of Paul, although he is a wonderful example of Christian behavior. We are followers of Jesus Christ and it is by His words that we want to live.

Further on in the New Testament, Paul writes: "All Scripture is given by God and is useful for teaching, for showing people what is wrong in their lives, for correcting faults, and for teaching how to live right. Using the

Scriptures, the person who serves God will be capable, having all that is needed to do every good work." II Timothy 3:16-17 (NCV). Peter tells us in II Peter 1:20-21 that Scripture is not man-made. Rather, it was written by "men moved by the Holy Spirit spoke from God."

With that almighty power in mind, we are cautioned not to misrepresent God's word. Anyone, even an angel from Heaven, who distorts the Gospel will be cursed and condemned, according to Galatians 1:8-9. Rather, we are to do as II Timothy 2:15 tells us and accurately handle the word of truth. Disciple and Gospel writer John asserts: "I warn everyone who hears the words of the prophecy of this book: If anyone adds anything to them, God will add to him the plagues described in this book. And if anyone takes words away from this book of prophecy, God will take away from him his share in the tree of life and in the holy city, which are described in this book." Revelation 22:18-19 (NIV).

Scripture tells us that God's word is right and true, and that wisdom and understanding are better than gold and silver. Despite those acclamations, we can still be nonchalant—even downright lazy—when it comes to reading the Bible. "Tomb Empty, Slain Christ Risen" is the headline of a lifetime that should compel us to read the whole story, but so many of us don't. We may be content with the biblical instruction we get at church. We may be intimidated, confused, or overwhelmed by where in this vast book to actually start reading. Or, as goal-oriented people, we may be discouraged that we will never get through the whole book with its small type, somewhat antiquated language, and delicate pages that seem hard to turn and easy to tear.

We may have a Bible that we consider a collectible keepsake, rather than a readable book. We may even wince when we hear the glue crack on the spine as we gently open the front cover, fearing we will spoil it. But just as soft and faded blue jeans identify them as our favorites, a well-worn

Bible should indicate how much it's used and enjoyed. We wouldn't demote the works of William Shakespeare or Jane Austen to a display-only shelf, and we shouldn't archive our Bibles either. God is pleased when we become habitual readers of His word. A dog-eared page does not offend Him.

One of the ways to make the Bible more accessible is to select a translation that best suits us. The Bible comes in many versions including the "New American Standard Bible," the "New Century Version," the "New International Version," the "New Living Translation," the "King James Version," and the "Living Bible." Although each has the same message and meaning, the "King James Version," for instance, uses a more formal prose than the "Living Bible," which uses a colloquial style. We may also choose a "study" Bible that includes detailed reference sections and footnotes to help direct us to, and explain particular verses and subjects. God communicates to us through the Bible. Let's see what He has to say.

Here are some other verses that emphasize why we need to know the power and wisdom of His word.

- "The counsel of the LORD stands forever, the plans of His heart from generation to generation." Psalm 33:11
- "How can a young man keep his way pure? By living according to your word." Psalm 119:9 (NIV)
- "Your word is a lamp to my feet and a light to my path." Psalm 119:105
- "…fools hate knowledge." Proverbs 1:22
- "Wise men store up knowledge..." Proverbs 10:14
- "How much better it is to get wisdom than gold! And to get understanding is to be chosen above silver." Proverbs 16:16
- "'And the LORD will continually guide you…'" Isaiah 58:11

- "`Is not my word like fire,' declares the LORD, `and like a hammer that breaks a rock in pieces?'" Jeremiah 23:29 (NIV)
- "`MAN SHALL NOT LIVE ON BREAD ALONE, BUT ON EVERY WORD THAT PROCEEDS OUT OF THE MOUTH OF GOD.'" Matthew 4:4 and Deuteronomy 8:3
- "`If you continue in My word, *then* you are truly disciples of Mine; and you will know the truth, and the truth will make you free.'" John 8:31-32
- "So faith *comes* from hearing, and hearing by the word of Christ." Romans 10:17
- "See to it that no one takes you captive through philosophy and empty deception, according to the tradition of men, according to the elementary principles of the world, rather than according to Christ." Colossians 2:8
- "Let the word of Christ dwell in you richly as you teach and admonish one another with all wisdom, and as you sing psalms, hymns and spiritual songs with gratitude in your hearts to God." Colossians 3:16 (NIV)
- "We must pay more careful attention, therefore, to what we have heard, so that we do not drift away." Hebrews 2:1 (NIV)
- "For the word of God is living and active and sharper than any two-edged sword, and piercing as far as the division of soul and spirit, of both joints and marrow, and able to judge the thoughts and intentions of the heart." Hebrews 4:12
- "You have been born again, and this new life did not come from something that dies, but from something that cannot die. You were born again through God's living message that continues forever. The Scripture says, `All people are like grass, and all their glory is like the flowers of the field. The grass dies and the flowers fall, but the

word of the Lord will live forever.′ And this is the word that was preached to you.” I Peter 1:23-25 (NCV)

CHAPTER III

Freed by Faith

It is very humbling to take an account of our shortcomings. It's unpleasant, but it's necessary. How can we ask God to forgive our sins if we refuse to recognize and acknowledge them? Paul advises us of this in I Corinthians 11:28 when he says that "a man must examine himself."

The Bible describes the numerous ways we sin—being unkind, jealous, unforgiving, prideful, malicious, or judgmental; lying; gossiping; stealing; having impure thoughts; etc. In other words, we have "the knowledge of sin," according to Romans 3:20. This realization of how sinful we are is not meant to belittle us, but to remind us of how different we are from God and our need for Christ as our atonement. "He made Him who knew no sin *to be* sin on our behalf, so that we might become the righteousness of God in Him." II Corinthians 5:21.

Let's picture God in Heaven and us far below Him, and a thick layer of sin in between. We need a way to get through that sinful matter so that we can ultimately be with Him in Heaven. That layer—for all of us—is just too dense to get through on our own.

We all know people who we think are "better" Christians than we are: they may be missionaries or clergy who are true, tireless, and self-sacrificing workers for the Lord and we assume that they have much thinner layers of sin than we do. They are great examples for us, yet like us, they are not saved by good works. Rather they are saved by their faith in Jesus and their good works are the product of that faith. "And without faith it is impossible to please *Him*..." Hebrews 11:6.

We want to do our best, certainly, and be progressive in our Christian behavior, but that's not the key to salvation. Even if we only committed one sin during the course of our lives, we would still be separated from God because He has committed *none*. "THERE IS NONE RIGHTEOUS, NOT EVEN ONE," Romans 3:10 tells us. "For all have sinned and fall short of the glory of God," continues Romans 3:23. "If we say that we have no sin, we are deceiving ourselves and the truth is not in us." I John 1:8.

But, if we are repentant and ask God to forgive our sins—believing that Christ has purified the polluted layer between us and God—and ask the Holy Spirit to come into our hearts, that barrier between us and the Lord will be lifted. "For `WHOEVER WILL CALL ON THE NAME OF THE LORD WILL BE SAVED,'" Romans 10:13 assures us. It's like Dorothy in the "Wizard of Oz;" she wanted to go home so badly. All she needed to do was to ask in faith and believe in the power that was there all along.

True Christian faith, at its highest level, is very personal. No one can give it to us and no one can take it from us. We do not inherit a saving faith from our parents; God does not have grandchildren. Believing in Christ as Savior is a conscious, thoughtful, and deliberate act that each of us has to do for ourselves. Jesus chooses those who choose Him. It's a reciprocal relationship. "But the man who loves God is known by God." I Corinthians 8:3 (NIV).

We must not forget that the Trinity includes Father, Son, *and* the Holy Spirit. They are three separate manifestations of one God—three sides of the triangle that are one complete shape. A triangle that is missing one side looks like a mathematical "less than" sign; and so it is true of our God who would be "less than" and incomplete as the Trinity without the Holy Spirit.

For instance, water, ice, and steam are three different forms of the same chemical substance. For that reason, we must also refer to the Spirit as "He," not as "it," just as we do the Father and the Son, and just as Jesus does in John 15:26 when He says, "'He will testify about Me.'" Jesus also refers to the Holy Spirit as "the Helper" and "the Spirit of truth," in that verse and in John 14:16-17, and as He who "will convict the world concerning sin and righteousness and judgment" in John 16:8. We must ask the Holy Spirit to descend upon us just as He did with Jesus, as described in Matthew 3:16, and as He did with the disciples in John 20:22, which says: Jesus "breathed on them and said to them, 'Receive the Holy Spirit.'"

As a helper, the Holy Spirit is an undeniable asset. While the *penalty* for our sins is ultimately met through Christ's death on the cross, the *power* of sin will be present in our lives until we are in Heaven with God. Sin will ever be an obstacle for all of us until the end of this age, but God sends the Holy Spirit into our hearts to help us overcome that sinful pull. "So, my brothers and sisters, we must not be ruled by our sinful selves or live the way our sinful selves want. If you use your lives to do the wrong things your sinful selves want, you will die spiritually. But if you use the Spirit's help to stop doing the wrong things you do with your body, you will have true life. The true children of God are those who let God's Spirit lead them." Romans 8:12-14 (NCV). In verse 26 of that chapter, we are told that the Holy Spirit helps us with our problems and weaknesses, and that He actually prays for us.

Paul cautions us in I Thessalonians 5:19 not to stifle or extinguish the Spirit. "If we live by the Spirit, let us also walk by the Spirit," he tells us in Galatians 5:25. That is wonderful advice as he describes the blessings or "fruit" of the Spirit in Galatians 5:22-23 as love, joy, peace, patience, kindness, goodness, faithfulness, gentleness, and self-control. Wouldn't we all be happier if we had bigger helpings of those qualities? The gifts or fruit of the Holy Spirit will vastly improve our lives and our ability to serve God. We should be hungry for them.

Believing in the Holy Spirit is essential in recognizing the fullness of who God really is; we cannot do without Him. "But when the kindness of God our Savior and *His* love for mankind appeared, He saved us, not on the basis of deeds which we have done in righteousness, but according to His mercy, by the washing of regeneration and renewing by the Holy Spirit, whom He poured out upon us richly through Jesus Christ our Savior." Titus 3:4-6.

Paul describes believers as being "sealed" in Christ with the Holy Spirit as a "pledge" of our inheritance in both Ephesians 1:13-14 and in II Corinthians 1:22. He tells us in Romans 8:9 and 11 that the Spirit *must* dwell in us to bind us to God and to ensure our eternity with Him. Paul concludes II Corinthians 13:14 with these loving words: "The grace of the Lord Jesus Christ, and the love of God, and the fellowship of the Holy Spirit, be with you all."

These Scriptures assure us that our faith in Jesus as our Redeemer reconciles us to God.

- "`Come to Me, all who are weary and heavy-laden, and I will give you rest. Take My yoke upon you and learn from Me, for I am gentle and humble in heart, and YOU WILL FIND REST FOR YOUR SOULS. For My yoke is easy and My burden is light.'" Matthew 11:28-30
- "`Thus it is written, that the Christ would suffer and rise again from the dead the third day, and that repentance for forgiveness of sins would be proclaimed in His name to all the nations, beginning from Jerusalem.'" Luke 24:46-47

- "`Behold, the Lamb of God who takes away the sin of the world!'" John 1:29
- "So that whoever believes will in Him have eternal life." John 3:15
- "Jesus answered and said to them, `This is the work of God, that you believe in Him whom He has sent.'" John 6:29
- "`Truly, truly, I say to you, he who believes has eternal life. I am the bread of life.'" John 6:47-48
- "`You are from below, I am from above; you are of this world, I am not of this world. Therefore I said to you that you will die in your sins; for unless you believe that I am *He*, you will die in your sins.'" John 8:23-24
- "`So if the Son makes you free, you will be free indeed.'" John 8:36
- "`I am the door; if anyone enters through Me, he will be saved…'" John 10:9
- "`I came that they may have life, and have *it* abundantly. I am the good shepherd; the good shepherd lays down His life for the sheep.'" John 10:10-11
- "`And I give eternal life to them, and they will never perish; and no one will snatch them out of My hand. My Father, who has given *them* to Me, is greater than all; and no one is able to snatch *them* out of the Father's hand. I and the Father are one.'" John 10:28-30
- "`I am the resurrection and the life; he who believes in Me will live even if he dies, and everyone who lives and believes in Me will never die.'" John 11:25-26
- "`I am the way, and the truth, and the life; no one comes to the Father but through Me.'" John 14:6
- "`These things I have spoken to you, so that in Me you may have peace. In the world you have

tribulation, but take courage; I have overcome the world.'" John 16:33

- "'Blessed *are* they who did not see, and *yet* believed.'" John 20:29
- "'And there is salvation in no one else; for there is no other name under heaven that has been given among men by which we must be saved.'" Acts 4:12
- "Therefore let it be known to you, brethren, that through Him forgiveness of sins is proclaimed to you." Acts 13:38
- "Therefore, having been justified by faith, we have peace with God through our Lord Jesus Christ." Romans 5:1
- "For while we were still helpless, at the right time Christ died for the ungodly." Romans 5:6
- "But God demonstrates His own love toward us, in that while we were yet sinners, Christ died for us." Romans 5:8
- "Now if we have died with Christ, we believe that we shall also live with Him, knowing that Christ, having been raised from the dead, is never to die again; death no longer is master over Him. For the death that He died, He died to sin, once for all; but the life that He lives, He lives to God. Even so consider yourselves to be dead to sin, but alive to God in Christ Jesus." Romans 6:8-11
- "For the wages of sin is death, but the free gift of God is eternal life in Christ Jesus our Lord." Romans 6:23
- "That if you confess with your mouth Jesus *as* Lord, and believe in your heart that God raised Him from the dead, you shall be saved." Romans 10:9
- "…in Christ all will be made alive." I Corinthians 15:22

- "'O DEATH, WHERE IS YOUR VICTORY? O DEATH, WHERE IS YOUR STING?'" I Corinthians 15:55
- "In him we have redemption through his blood, the forgiveness of sins, in accordance with the riches of God's grace that he lavished on us with all wisdom and understanding." Ephesians 1:7-8 (NIV)
- "But God, being rich in mercy, because of His great love with which He loved us, even when we were dead in our transgressions, made us alive together with Christ (by grace you have been saved)." Ephesians 2:4-5
- "For by grace you have been saved through faith; and that not of yourselves, *it is* the gift of God; not as a result of works, so that no one may boast." Ephesians 2:8-9
- "So that at the name of Jesus EVERY KNEE WILL BOW, of those who are in heaven and on earth and under the earth, and that every tongue will confess that Jesus Christ is Lord, to the glory of God the Father." Philippians 2:10-11
- "Therefore as you have received Christ Jesus the Lord, *so* walk in Him, having been firmly rooted *and now* being built up in Him and established in your faith, just as you were instructed, *and* overflowing with gratitude....For in Him all the fullness of Deity dwells in bodily form, and in Him you have been made complete, and He is the head over all rule and authority." Colossians 2:6, 7, 9 and 10
- "The Son is the radiance of God's glory and the exact representation of his being, sustaining all things by his powerful word. After he had provided purification for sins, he sat down at the right hand of the Majesty in heaven." Hebrews 1:3 (NIV)
- "And though you have not seen Him, you love Him, and though you do not see Him now, but

believe in Him, you greatly rejoice with joy inexpressible and full of glory, obtaining as the outcome of your faith the salvation of your souls." I Peter 1:8-9

- "But you are A CHOSEN RACE, A ROYAL PRIESTHOOD, A HOLY NATION, A PEOPLE FOR GOD'S OWN POSSESSION, so that you may proclaim the excellencies of Him who has called you out of darkness into His marvelous light; for you once were NOT A PEOPLE, but now you are THE PEOPLE OF GOD; you had NOT RECEIVED MERCY, but now you have RECEIVED MERCY." I Peter 2:9-10
- "If we confess our sins, He is faithful and righteous to forgive us our sins and to cleanse us from all unrighteousness." I John 1:9
- "And the testimony is this, that God has given us eternal life, and this life is in His Son. He who has the Son has the life; he who does not have the Son of God does not have the life." I John 5:11-12

CHAPTER IV

He So Loves the World

When we take up the cross of Christ, we must follow Him in His message of love for *all* people. Jesus tells us this so succinctly in John 3:16: "'For God so loved the world, that He gave His only begotten Son, that whoever believes in Him shall not perish, but have eternal life.'" Accordingly, we must love *all* of the world's people—Muslims, Hindus, Buddhists, Jews, and anyone else who does not worship Jesus as we do—for whom God sent His Son.

People who have grown up in different religious backgrounds and who have never heard the Gospel are in God's hands, and we can be sure that He will do right by them. "'...For God *sees* not as man sees, for man looks at the outward appearance, but the LORD looks at the heart.'" I Samuel 16:7.

It is imperative that we remember that the non-believer is just as good as those of us who profess to be Christians. Ephesians 6:9 tells us that "there is no partiality with Him." Peter says in Acts 10:34-35: "'I most certainly understand *now* that God is not one to show partiality, but in every nation the man who fears Him and does what is right is welcome to Him.'" God repeatedly tells us throughout the Bible that He gives love, mercy, and salvation to "us" and to the "world." Both words are all-inclusive and don't distinguish between those who don't know Him yet, and those who do. We are all His creations and therefore equal in His perfect eyes. "This is how God showed his love among us: He sent his one and only Son into the world that we might live through him....We love because he first loved us." I John 4: 9 and 19 (NIV).

As Jesus' followers, we are expected to have the same equity in our compassion and love for others. Leviticus 19:18 tells us "`you shall love your neighbor as yourself; I am the LORD.'" If this seems like an impossible task, remember that the verse ends with "I am the LORD." In other words, what we cannot do by ourselves, we *can* do with the help of God.

"You shall love you neighbor as yourself" is also repeated in the following eight verses in the New Testament: Matthew 5:43, Matthew 19:19, Matthew 22:39, Mark 12:31, Luke 10:27, Romans 13:9, Galatians 5:14, and James 2:8. The Greek word for love used in each of those verses and in the Greek (from the original Hebrew) translation of Leviticus 19:18 is the same—*agape.* Agape is a commanded, unconditional love. It means to love dearly or have universal goodwill toward others. It is not an *if* and *when* kind of love that allows us to postpone loving others until *if* and *when* we deem them worthy; it places no conditions on the recipients to change in order to be loved. Rather, it is an absolute, total, and unlimited kind of love that applies to everyone regardless of race, color, or religious background.

It's easy to love people who love us back, to serve those who serve us in return, and to give to those who give to us. The challenge is to love people who annoy us, who are rude or mean to us, or who just plain rub us the wrong way; but that is exactly what God wants us to do. "`But love your enemies, and do good, and lend, expecting nothing in return; and your reward will be great, and you will be sons of the Most High; for He Himself is kind to ungrateful and evil *men*. Be merciful, just as your Father is merciful.'" Luke 6:35-36.

We must never forget that we are all brothers and sisters because of one simple fact—we have the same Heavenly Father. "And this commandment we have from Him, that the one who loves God should love his brother also," I John 4:21 tells us. With that kinship in mind, we must follow the Golden Rule in all of our interactions. "'Treat people the same way you want them to treat you.'" Jesus says in Matthew 7:12 and Luke 6:31.

Jesus met with sinners in order to heal them physically, mentally, and spiritually; but, He knew that their greatest need was spiritual cleansing. That is why He told the accusers of an adulterous woman—who intended to stone her to death for her misdeeds—to consider this: "'He who is without sin among you, let him *be the* first to throw a stone at her.'" John 8:7. After they realized that their own sins made them unworthy of such judgment, Jesus told the woman: "'I do not condemn you, either. Go. From now on sin no more.'" John 8:11. Jesus was a man of new beginnings who knew that people needed to get beyond their pasts. "'For God did not send the Son into the world to judge the world, but that the world might be saved through Him.'" John 3:17.

Jesus was more concerned about comforting the sinner than condemning his sin. Immediately after He rose from the dead, Jesus told Mary Magdalene and Mary the mother of James to tell His disciples—and He specifically singles out Peter—that He has risen. He was concerned about Peter, who was ashamed that he had lied and denied knowing Jesus after He was arrested, and not about Peter's mistakes. He didn't take the first opportunity to make Peter feel worse, rather He chose to reassure and encourage Peter as soon as He got the chance. We are healed by His wounds, according to I Peter 2:24, "so that we might die to sin and live to righteousness."

The word "evangelical" is supposed to describe something that is wonderful. It has to do with "good news." In the Christian context it has to do with the Gospel—sharing the Good News about God's love for us and the sacrifice Jesus made for us on the cross. Sadly, today's evangelicals can be viewed by the man on the street as mean, legalistic, and judgmental. That is not what Christianity is all about! There is absolutely no place for meanness in the Christian life.

"Do you not know that you are a temple of God and *that* the Spirit of God dwells in you?" Paul asks in I Corinthians 3:16. How, then, can we possibly justify being unkind to anyone? We wouldn't expect a house that is beautifully appointed on the inside to be dilapidated on the outside. As the Lord's dwelling, we need to have some curb appeal by making sure that our inward acceptance of God's Holy Spirit shows in our behavior. We are vessels of His Spirit; there is no more precious cargo. We need to lovingly and graciously deliver the goods.

Bullying, shaming, criticizing, and acting holier than others must become obsolete if we are to become worthy advertisers of the Gospel. As Christians, we should feel so loved, confident, and peaceful that our declaration for Christ is infectious and encouraging. We need to avoid being conceited saints who are quick to judge and remember that we are convicted sinners who have been mercifully forgiven.

"'Do not judge so that you will not be judged,'" Jesus tells us. "'For in the way you judge, you will be judged; and by your standard of measure, it will be measured to you. Why do you look at the speck that is in your brother's eye, but do not notice the log that is in your own eye?'" Matthew 7:1-3.

These verses also tell us that we should emulate God's unconditional love for all humankind.

- "Above all, keep fervent in your love for one another, because love covers a multitude of sins. Be hospitable to one another without complaint." I Peter 4:8-9
- "The one who says he is in the Light and *yet* hates his brother is in the darkness until now. The one who loves his brother abides in the Light and there is no cause for stumbling in him." I John 2:9-10
- "We know love by this, that He laid down His life for us; and we ought to lay down our lives for the brethren." I John 3:16
- "Beloved, let us love one another, for love is from God; and everyone who loves is born of God and knows God." I John 4:7
- "Beloved, if God so loved us, we also ought to love one another." I John 4:11
- "And we have come to know and have believed the love which God has for us. God is love, and the one who abides in love abides in God, and God abides in him." I John 4:16

CHAPTER V
Be Baptized

The role of baptism in Christian conversion can be a contentious topic among believers. When and how we should be baptized elicits varying views, but the Bible offers us consistent advice on the matter. God's word should convict us of what baptism really means.

Our primary example, as always, is the Lord Jesus who was immersed in the Jordan River by John the Baptist. "Now when all the people were baptized, Jesus was also baptized, and while He was praying, heaven was opened, and the Holy Spirit descended upon Him in bodily form like a dove, and a voice came out of heaven, `You are My beloved Son, in You I am well-pleased.'" Luke 3:21-22, Matthew 3:16-17, and Mark 1:10-11.

Although Jesus was sinless and did not require baptism, He was immersed as an example for all of us to follow. "`He who has believed and been baptized shall be saved; but he who has disbelieved shall be condemned,'" Jesus says in Mark 16:16. "`Go therefore and make disciples of all the nations, baptizing them in the name of the Father and the Son and the Holy Spirit,'" He tells us in Matthew 28:19.

After Paul (then called Saul) met Jesus on the road to Damascus, he converted and was soon told by a righteous man named Ananias, "'Now why do you delay? Get up and be baptized, and wash away your sins, calling on His name.'" Acts 22:16. Paul tells us later in Galatians 3:27, "For all of you who were baptized into Christ have clothed yourselves with Christ."

Baptism is an act of obedience that demonstrates confirmation of our faith. It is an act of allegiance to our commander, Jesus, and when we love Him, we gladly do what He asks of us. We have been "buried with Him in baptism" in which we were also "raised up with Him through faith in the working of God, who raised Him from the dead," according to Colossians 2:12.

Peter describes how Noah, his wife, his three sons, and their wives—only eight people—"were saved through water, and this water symbolizes baptism that now saves you also—not the removal of dirt from the body but the pledge of a good conscience toward God. It saves you by the resurrection of Jesus Christ, who has gone into heaven and is at God's right hand—with angels, authorities and powers in submission to him." I Peter 3:20-22 (NIV).

Peter also tells new followers that they must believe and be baptized. Note how belief always comes first and then the act of baptism. Acts 2:38 and 41 tell us: "'Repent, and each of you be baptized in the name of Jesus Christ for the forgiveness of your sins; and you will receive the gift of the Holy Spirit....' So then, those who had received his word were baptized; and that day there were added about three thousand souls." While Peter was preaching at Caesarea, "the Holy Spirit fell upon those who were listening to the message." Peter then says: "'Surely no one can refuse the water for these to be baptized who have received the Holy Spirit just as we *did,* can he?' And he ordered them to be baptized in the name of Jesus Christ." Acts 10:44, 47-48.

These Scriptures also confirm that conversion always *precedes* baptism.

- The disciple Philip was preaching in the city of Samaria. "But when they believed Philip preaching the good news about the kingdom of God and the name of Jesus Christ, they were being baptized, men and women alike. Even Simon (a sorcerer) himself believed; and after being baptized, he continued on with Philip, and as he observed signs and great miracles taking place, he was constantly amazed." Acts 8:12-13
- The disciple Philip also baptized an Ethiopian eunuch after he confessed Christ as Savior. Acts 8:37-38
- A woman named Lydia was converted after listening to Paul speak about Jesus, and then she and her household were baptized. Acts 16:14-15
- The jailer who held Paul and Silas prisoners, and his household became Christians and were baptized "immediately." Acts 16:31-33
- "Crispus, the leader of the synagogue, believed in the Lord with all his household, and many of the Corinthians when they heard were believing and being baptized." Acts 18:8

CHAPTER VI

Proclaim Him

Once we have made a decision for Christ, we must faithfully and lovingly share His message of salvation with others. We are not responsible for the response we get from others, as Matthew 10:14 tells us, but we are responsible for doing the sharing, as Matthew 10:5-42 details. Christ tells us to boldly proclaim His truth, just as He told His followers 2,000 years ago: "'Go into all the world and preach the gospel to all creation.'" Mark 16:15. He tells His disciples that they are to be His witnesses in Jerusalem, in all of Judea and Samaria, and even in "the remotest part of the earth" in Acts 1:8. "'As the Father has sent Me, I also send you,'" He says in John 20:21.

Evangelism is the faithful, enthusiastic presentation of the Gospel of Jesus Christ to the unsaved. Many Christians have a desire to be soul-winners, but say they don't know how. They are afraid of failure so they sit back and allow the "professional clergy" to do the actual work of evangelism. They are afraid of not being able to answer the questions posed to them.

Moses had the same lack of confidence in his ability to articulate God's message to his fellow Hebrews, as well as to the Egyptian Pharaoh who had enslaved them. He describes himself in Exodus 4:10 as "slow of speech and slow of tongue" and asks God to appoint another spokesman. But God never gives His people a task to perform without providing the means to accomplish it and He promises Moses that He will teach him what to say.

Despite God's encouragement, Moses is still unable to overcome his fear of effectively delivering God's words and the job goes to his older brother, Aaron. But God doesn't give up on Moses. Even though Aaron becomes the messenger, God continues to speak through Moses. In Exodus 4:15 (NIV), God reassures Moses of His guidance telling him, "`I will help both of you speak and will teach you what to do.'"

The Bible repeatedly tells us that God will help us as we represent Him. Isaiah was eager to spread God's word, as he tells us in Isaiah 6:8: "`Here am I. Send me!'" He knew that God would help him do just that. "`I have put My words in your mouth,'" God says in Isaiah 51:16. The Lord also promises that His word will be effective: "`It will not return to me empty, but will accomplish what I desire and achieve the purpose for which I sent it.'" Isaiah 55:11 (NIV).

The New Testament also assures us that the Holy Spirit will guide us as we speak on God's behalf. In Matthew 10:20, Jesus tells His disciples, "`For it is not you who speak, but *it is* the Spirit of your Father who speaks in you.'" In Luke 12:11-12, Jesus tells us not to be anxious about sharing our faith and defending Him because the Holy Spirit will teach us what to say. Again, in Luke 21:15, Jesus says, "`For I will give you utterance and wisdom which none of your opponents will be able to resist or refute.'" And in John 14:26 He tells us that "`the Helper, the Holy Spirit, whom the Father will send in My name, He will teach you all things, and bring to you remembrance all that I said to you.'" However, we need to study what Jesus actually did say so that we can accurately testify for Him.

Examining our own story of how we came to know Christ and why we believe in Him gives us an example to share with others. Our declaration for Jesus, supported by the biblical truth that prompted our own faith, is a mighty story. Let's make it mightier still by being well-read and well-prepared in our knowledge of God's word so that we can more effectively share the Good News.

"Therefore, we are ambassadors for Christ, as though God were making an appeal through us; we beg you on behalf of Christ, be reconciled to God." II Corinthians 5:20. As Christ's agents, let's do our best to eloquently describe Him. "For I am not ashamed of the gospel, for it is the power of God for salvation to everyone who believes." Romans 1:16.

We must remember that we are to represent Christ in both deed and words *lovingly*. People need to know how much we care, before they will care about how much we know. Luke records the story of some men who were carrying their paralyzed friend on a bed to where Jesus was teaching indoors, hoping that Jesus would heal the man. "But not finding any *way* to bring him in because of the crowd, they went up on the roof and let him down through the tiles with his stretcher, into the middle *of the crowd,* in front of Jesus. Seeing their faith, He said, `Friend, your sins are forgiven you.'" Luke 5:19-20. "Immediately he got up before them, and picked up what he had been lying on, and went home glorifying God." Luke 5:25. When is the last time we tore the roof off of a building to put a friend in the presence of Christ?

We must start with people where we find them, not where we want them to be. They may be fooled by the Devil—literally the world's biggest liar who Jesus describes in John 8:44 as "the father of lies"—into thinking that they are unworthy of salvation. They may have been rejected by people who were supposed to love them—their parents, a spouse, or friends—and cannot comprehend Christ's remarkable and unconditional love for them. They may think they are "worth less" than others or just plain "worthless," both of which are dangerous lies asserted by our vicious opponent—the Devil.

We must make it emphatically clear that God has the exact opposite opinion of His beloved creations and that absolutely nothing can separate us from Christ's love. "For I am convinced that neither death, nor life, nor angels, nor principalities, nor things present, nor things to come, nor powers, nor height, nor depth, nor any other created thing, will be able to separate us from the love of God, which is in Christ Jesus our Lord." Romans 8:38-39.

Peoples' imperfection is bound to disappoint us, but Christ's perfection never will. "Jesus Christ *is* the same yesterday and today and forever," Hebrews 13:8 tells us. He loves us, blemishes and all, and that will never change, no matter how ugly, unpopular, or unlovable we may feel. John tells us that God's love and power make each of us a winning majority against the enemy. "…Greater is He who is in you than he who is in the world," he says in I John 4:4. "If God *is* for us, who *is* against us?" asks Romans 8:31. We must never underestimate or doubt God's infinite ability and desire to demolish evil. "Put on the full armor of God, so that you will be able to stand firm against the schemes of the devil. For our struggle is not against flesh and blood, but against the rulers, against the powers, against the world forces of this darkness, against the spiritual *forces* of wickedness in the heavenly *places*." Ephesians 6:11-12.

The Devil may also fool people into thinking that they are too sinful to be saved by Christ, that Christ came for just some and not all of mankind, or that he simply does not exist and therefore does not need to be feared. Those are all lies! Certainly Satan exists! John refers to him in Revelation 12:9 as "the serpent of old who is called the devil and Satan, who deceives the whole world."

Remember him in the Garden of Eden disguised as a serpent goading Adam and Eve into mankind's first sin?

He was also with Jesus in the wilderness to tempt Him away from God the Father. "Again, the devil took Him to a very high mountain and showed Him all the kingdoms of the world and their glory; and he said to Him, `All these things will I give You, if You fall down and worship me.' Then Jesus said to him, `Go, Satan! For it is written, `YOU SHALL WORSHIP THE LORD YOUR GOD, AND SERVE HIM ONLY,'" Matthew 4:8-10 says, as do Mark 1:12-13 and Luke 4:5-8.

Rest assured, our perfect God does not lie, as Paul tells us in Titus 1:2. It is actually "impossible for God to lie," according to Hebrews 6:18. Lying is sinful and God does not sin. So, when He tells us that He loves us, and has died and risen to set us free from our sins, we must believe Him. Hallelujah! That is the kind of news that must be shared! Daniel 12:3 (NCV) tells us that "Those who teach others to live right will shine like stars forever and ever."

CHAPTER VII

Unfailing Forgiveness

"'And forgive us our debts, as we also have forgiven our debtors.'" Matthew 6:12. Some people are easier to forgive than others, just as some people are easier to love than others. But that doesn't mean we can be selective about who we love and who we forgive. Christ forgave us *all,* and as He is our example, we must too. "Be kind to one another, tender-hearted, forgiving each other, just as God in Christ also has forgiven you." Ephesians 4:32.

For most of us, that is a huge task that seems nearly impossible. Does God realize what He is asking? Does He know how terrible some people have been to us? Sure He does! Look at how people have treated Him and He is perfect! Not only is our forgiveness of others an act of obedience, but our forgiveness releases us from anger and frustration.

Our all-knowing God knows that our disappointment and resentment toward others can cripple us. He doesn't want us to be consumed and embittered by those painful feelings, so He tells us to give it to Him in prayer. We will face challenging people throughout our lives; anger will exhaust us if we don't forgive them. Peter asks Jesus in Matthew 18:21-22: "`Lord, how often shall my brother sin against me and I forgive him? Up to seven times?' Jesus said to him, `I do not say to you, up to seven times, but up to seventy times seven.'"

Jesus also tells us in Matthew 5:44 and again in Luke 6:27-28 that we must love our enemies, pray for those who persecute us, and bless and be kind to those who curse us. "`Whoever hits you on the cheek, offer him the other also,'" He says in Luke 6:29. If that sounds too unbearable, consider the consequences of retaliating against someone's anger. When we treat people with sensitivity and tact, we can often smooth over a bad situation. It takes at least two to tangle. Proverbs 29:8 tells us that "wise men turn away anger." Proverbs 6:16 and 19 tell us that God actually "hates" it when someone "spreads strife among brothers." If we engage an aggressor, we generally compound bad feelings and magnify the problem. God doesn't want us to live like that. Turning the other cheek is not only a loving act toward our enemies, but it benefits us too by promoting peace, not perpetuating conflict. "`Blessed are the peacemakers, for they shall be called sons of God,'" Jesus tells us in Matthew 5:9. Christ came to give us an abundant life, not one full of tension, broken relationships, and burnt bridges.

"`For if you forgive others for their transgressions, your heavenly Father will also forgive you. But if you do not forgive others, then your Father will not forgive your transgressions,'" Jesus says in Matthew 6:14-15. "`Do not judge, and you will not be judged; and do not condemn, and you will not be condemned; pardon, and you will be pardoned,'" He tells us in Luke 6:37.

We may not always pray for our enemies with a willing or sincere heart. We may initially pray for them with clenched teeth and fists simply as an act of obedience to God. But praying for God to help us forgive our enemies—a parent, a sibling, an in-law, a step-parent, a boss, a coworker, a former spouse or friend, or a perpetrator of some kind—and for them to know Christ as Savior is a remarkable salve for *us*. Praying for someone is an act of love, and when we do it, it bears the fruit of peace in us. God will soften our hearts through those prayers; when we ask Him to replace hate and anger with compassion and understanding, He will. "I can do all things through Him who strengthens me." Philippians 4:13.

Forgiveness allows us to move forward, and not be slowed or preoccupied by vengeful feelings. It also allows us to take assessing the condemnation and punishment of others off of our to-do list. We can leave those determinations up to God, who will do an appreciably better job in dispensing justice. James 4:12 reminds us that "There is *only* one Lawgiver and Judge, the One who is able to save and to destroy; but who are you who judge your neighbor?"

The story of the notorious cities of Sodom and Gomorrah, whose citizens' sin is described as "exceedingly grave," tells us that God certainly distinguishes between good and evil men, and responds equitably. Only a man named Lot (Abraham's nephew) is found worthy among the Sodomites to be spared, and he and his family are led out of the city by two angels before the Lord destroys it with fire and brimstone. (Lot's wife, however, disobeys the warning of one of the angel's who tells her not to look back at the city as they leave and she turns into a pillar of salt for her mistake.) Certainly the Judge of all the earth will deal justly, as Genesis 18:25 tells us, and He will not treat the righteous and the wicked alike.

We should be grateful and relieved to yield to God's just and true management. We have neither the authority nor the wisdom to replace Him as judge. Romans 12:17 and 19 advise us: "Never pay back evil for evil to anyone….Never take your own revenge, beloved, but leave room for the wrath *of God,* for it is written, `VENGEANCE IS MINE, I WILL REPAY,' says the Lord."

CHAPTER VIII

Clearly Christ's

Our love for non-Christians should always motivate us to behave in a way that does not hinder our testimony for Jesus Christ. Out of this love, we should ask ourselves if the choices we are making could possibly deny a lost soul access to Heaven. We don't want our words or actions to confuse non-Christians—whom we hope to encourage to know the Lord—by placing doubt in their minds about the appropriateness of our behavior. This is also important in our example to new Christians.

New or non-Christians sometimes hold proclaiming Christians to a higher standard of right and wrong than what is actually found in the Bible. Out of love for them, we should forgo certain habits or actions that may appear wrong so we do not mislead them. "But take care that this liberty of yours does not somehow become a stumbling block to the weak." I Corinthians 8:9.

The fourteenth chapter of Romans also repeatedly cautions us on this point. Verse 13 tells us that we are "not to put an obstacle or a stumbling block in a brother's way." Verse 21 reiterates this by saying that we should not do anything that causes a brother to feel unsteady or fall. In other words, "Love does no wrong to a neighbor," Romans 13:10 tells us.

For instance, we might need to curb our sense of competition in both work and play if it makes us appear dishonest, arrogant, or unkind. Maybe we should revise our definition of winning. Let's not be so ruthless about surpassing our co-workers, so haughty about one-upping our neighbors, or so zealous about reciting our children's accomplishments that we seem nasty, obnoxious, or boastful. We don't want to ignite a sinful reaction from others by making them feel defensive, uncomfortable, or angry. If we insist upon doing what we want, despite it being a catalyst to sin for a weaker brother or sister, it ceases to be just a matter of our opinion; it then becomes sin because we have wounded the conscience of others. When you sin against your brother, "you sin against Christ." I Corinthians 8:12.

Often things that do not appear right or wrong on the surface become wrong if they cause others to make bad choices. Those behaviors then become sinful if they cause non-believers, or weak or new Christians to fall back into their old ways of life. Sometimes it's just a matter of being thoughtful in somewhat ordinary circumstances, such as not pressuring someone to go out when we know that he is needed at home or not tempting a friend to buy something when we know that her finances are tight. We don't want to lead others into irresponsible behaviors, or bad situations or habits, even if they seem minor to us. We shouldn't make ourselves frantic about everything we do, but we need to be sensitive to what might trouble others and act accordingly.

We also want to be good Christian examples when we do routine activities. Let's not be the patron who prays before a meal and then scolds the waiter, or the driver who makes disparaging gestures, or the customer who acts superior to the store clerk. Hypocritical behavior belies motivated Christian love. We may feel anonymous and therefore less liable when we offend strangers, but we are called to be nice to everyone, even if we don't know them. We are not entitled to ruin someone's day because we can't find joy in ours. Our faith should compel us to be positive and pleasant even in seemingly small interactions. We are always witnesses and examples of Christ's love—even when we're doing errands. Let's try to discipline our moods and actions so that we encourage the new, non- or even long-time Christian to see who encourages us—Jesus!

If there is a serious question in our minds about a choice we are considering, there should be no question in our minds as to what to do. Therefore, if we cannot do it with an absolute good conscience, we should not do it at all. For instance, we might try to convince ourselves that we are only telling "little white lies" when we lie or that we are only "venting" when we gossip. But, we are more than likely just renaming sinful behaviors so that we can still do them without feeling quite so sinful. Euphemizing sin doesn't make it better; it just fools us into thinking that we don't have to be responsible for it. James 4:17 warns us: "Therefore, to one who knows *the* right thing to do and does not do it, to him it is sin." Romans 14:23 wisely counsels that "whatever is not from faith is sin."

God knows our hearts. For us to do something or make a decision that might not be pleasing to God is wrong. In other words, we shouldn't violate our consciences. That is why it is so important that our thinking is guided by good, sound biblical principles. Biblical knowledge gives us a better-informed, more God-directed conscience. "'Blessed are those who hear the word of God and observe it,'" Jesus tells us in Luke 11:28.

No matter how sincere we may be about something, it isn't right unless it's based on a solid foundation of facts. Although they are similar in meaning, "sincerity" and "truth" are not interchangeable words. Sincerity is a genuine or honest feeling; it is an emotion. Truth is fact, plain and simple; it is certainty and reality. We may sincerely *feel* something is logical, but in reality it will be wrong if it's based on a faulty major premise. Sometimes our gut feelings mislead us. Just ask any gambler whose horse didn't win the race or any broker whose stock recommendations didn't appreciate. The truth is the truth even if we try to ignore or defy it.

We are self-conscious beings with the ability to consider intelligently the consequences of our actions. That is what makes us accountable. Unfortunately, we often disregard the inevitable effects of what we shouldn't do and we do it anyway. God has given us the freedom to make choices, but He has not given us the freedom to choose their outcome. Whether we like it or not, we have to live with the results of our bad decisions. "For whatever a man sows, this he will also reap." Galatians 6:7.

God loves us all, sinners that we are, but He hates our sin because it destroys our relationships and our happiness. He encourages us to live good lives because He loves us. King David experienced the painful results of his sin after he committed adultery with a beautiful woman named Bathsheba and then sent her husband into the front line of battle to die so that he could marry her. "But the thing that David had done was evil in the sight of the LORD," says II Samuel 11:27. God punished David by allowing the son that resulted from the affair to die. Not only did King David suffer dearly for his sins of adultery and murder, but his actions had devastating consequences for his beloved wife, Bathsheba.

And so it is with us. Our sin not only causes disharmony and chaos in our own lives, but it has heartbreaking effects on those we love the most. Consider the substance abuser's impact on his family and friends. Frustration, disappointment, stress, and worry—even physical and financial ruin—can be the by-products of the addict's behavior on his loved ones.

The Devil has a way of blinding us to everything but the immediate pleasure of sin. He does not want us to see the future consequences. He can get us into Hell, but he cannot get us out. “There is a way *which seems* right to a man, but its end is the way of death.” Proverbs 14:12. “Submit therefore to God. Resist the devil and he will flee from you. Draw near to God and He will draw near to you.” James 4:7-8.

There is no better example of this than the inception of Original Sin by Adam and Eve. They had everything they could possibly need for a wonderful life in the Garden of Eden and blessed fellowship with God. All they had to do was avoid touching or eating the fruit of just one tree. But the Devil’s double-talking recast the forbidden tree of knowledge of good and evil into simply just a tree of knowledge that would put Adam and Eve on intellectual par with God. Eve heard a lie, she believed a lie, and she obeyed a lie. That brought death. We don’t become like God through disobedience. We become like Him through obedience. We need to hear the truth, believe the truth, and obey the truth. That brings life.

We must never be ashamed of doing what God commands us to do and not doing what He forbids us to do. When we accept Jesus as our Savior, we do have our sins forgiven, but that is just the beginning of the Christian life. We are expected to live a rich, full life of love and service to both God and His creation—man. We then need to be effectual doers of the word and not forgetful hearers of the word, according to James 1:25. Those words are echoed throughout chapter 2 where James tells us that “faith without works is dead.” James 2:26.

Scriptural faith demands obedience. We cannot merely accept the fact that Christ is our Savior intellectually—even if we believe fervently—without backing up our thoughts and feelings with actions.

These Scriptures remind us that our behavior should exemplify our faith in Christ.

- “How blessed are those who keep justice, who practice righteousness at all times!” Psalm 106:3

- "In all your ways acknowledge Him, and He will make your paths straight." Proverbs 3:6
- "'...blessed are they who keep my ways.'" Proverbs 8:32
- "'Blessed is the man who listens to me...'" Proverbs 8:34
- "'Anyone who breaks one of the least of these commandments and teaches others to do the same will be called least in the kingdom of heaven, but whoever practices and teaches these commands will be called great in the kingdom of heaven.'" Matthew 5:19 (NIV)
- "'If you know these things, you are blessed if you do them.'" John 13:17
- "Let us not lose heart in doing good, for in due time we will reap if we do not grow weary." Galatians 6:9
- "Finally, brethren, whatever is true, whatever is honorable, whatever is right, whatever is pure, whatever is lovely, whatever is of good repute, if there is any excellence and if anything worthy of praise, dwell on these things." Philippians 4:8
- "And as for you, brothers, never tire of doing what is right." II Thessalonians 3:13 (NIV)
- "In all things show yourself to be an example of good deeds, *with* purity in doctrine, dignified, sound *in* speech which is beyond reproach..." Titus 2:7-8

CHAPTER IX

Make Good Company

Although Scripture should always be our primary advisor, it is also helpful in decision-making to seek the counsel of people who have walked the Christian walk for many years—people we love and respect, people who lead by example, people who have demonstrated that they are good and faithful Christians by both their words and deeds, people who practice what they preach, and people who are motivated by Scripture. Then, with their counsel, we may become like what we see in them. "Spend time with the wise and you will become wise, but the friends of fools will suffer." Proverbs 13:20 (NCV). "How blessed is the man who does not walk in the counsel of the wicked," advises Psalm 1:1.

We may be blessed by a parent, grandparent, aunt, older sibling, or family friend who provides this godly example, and who has learned from the good, but hard teacher—experience. To help us avoid making wrong choices, they will tell us what we need to hear and not what we want to hear. Learned mentors are not afraid to ask the tough questions and hold us accountable for our actions. They have a burning desire to keep us from doing anything that could haunt us for the rest of our days. They urge us to focus on God's will for us so that we don't make today's foolishness tomorrow's regrets. "My son, do not forget my teaching, but keep my commands in your heart, for they will prolong your life many years and bring you prosperity," the wise King Solomon (second son of King David and Bathsheba) tells us in Proverbs 3:1-2 (NIV).

Good advisers help us determine and pursue right over wrong. They too rely on the Bible as their counsel and may remind us of what Psalm 32:10 warns: "Many are the sorrows of the wicked, but he who trusts in the LORD, lovingkindness shall surround him." Although God and His word are our definitive counselors, it is a blessed necessity to have a truthful mentor with whom we can have fellowship.

We should also be mindful of who we choose as friends. We are never supposed to be snobs, and we must always treat everyone with love and respect. However, we must not put ourselves in constant contact and fellowship with people whose influence on us might be bad. II Peter 3:17 tells us to be on our guard or we will risk being caught up in "the error of unprincipled men" and fall down ourselves. We must remember that wrong is still wrong even if everybody is doing it, and right is still right even if nobody is doing it. Isaiah spoke of this more than 2,700 years ago when he told us, "Woe to those who call evil good, and good evil." Isaiah 5:20. Paul tells us in Romans 12:9 to "abhor what is evil; cling to what is good."

Although we want to be encouraging and helpful to those who are struggling, we must be careful not to allow ourselves to be shadily influenced by others in order to be accepted. "Do not be deceived: `Bad company corrupts good morals,'" I Corinthians 15:33 says. We must immediately declare ourselves for Christ so there is no doubt as to who we are and what our basic values are. We are to "walk in the way of good men and keep to the paths of the righteous." Proverbs 2:20.

This also holds true for dating. We should be careful about who we date, and know something about him or her and his or her family. Once there was a farmer who raised pure-bred cattle, pigs, and sheep. He knew everything possible about their breeding. A friend asked him, "Whose boy is that your daughter is dating?" A blank look came over his face. He didn't have a clue. He knew the sires of his farm animals, but not who his own daughter was dating. That ought not to be so!

Our friends can either encourage us to live better or encourage us to live worse. A good and true friend brings out the best in us. Our peers have a tremendous influence on us, especially when we are young and more vulnerable to their suggestions. It's no coincidence that young people tend to dress alike, listen to the same kind of music, wear similar hairstyles, and use the same slang and inflection in their speech. But they need to be careful not to mimic their peers' unhealthy, illegal, or unbecoming habits in order to fit in. If our friends tempt us to do bad things, we need new friends. King Solomon warns us, "My son, if sinners entice you, do not consent....My son, do not walk in the way with them. Keep your feet from their path, for their feet run to evil." Proverbs 1:10 and 15-16. He also challenges us with these questions: "Can a man take fire in his bosom and his clothes not be burned? Or can a man walk on hot coals and his feet not be scorched?" Proverbs 6:27-28.

The great paradox of Christianity is that as Christians we are *in* the world, but not *of* the world. It's okay for the ship to be in the ocean, but it's not okay for the ocean to be in the ship. We are to keep ourselves "unstained by the world," according to James 1:27.

Consider carefully the words of Romans 12:2: "And do not be conformed to this world, but be transformed by the renewing of your mind, so that you may prove what the will of God is, that which is good and acceptable and perfect." The Lord tells us in II Corinthians 6:17 to "'COME OUT FROM THEIR MIDST AND BE SEPARATE.'"

"Do not love the world nor the things in the world. If anyone loves the world, the love of the Father is not in him. For all that is in the world, the lust of the flesh and the lust of the eyes and the boastful pride of life, is not from the Father, but is from the world. The world is passing away, and *also* its lusts; but the one who does the will of God lives forever." I John 2:15-17. "Rather, clothe yourselves with the Lord Jesus Christ, and do not think about how to gratify the desires of the sinful nature." Romans 13:14 (NIV).

Jesus tells us in John 14:27: "'Peace I leave with you; My peace I give to you; not as the world gives do I give to you. Do not let your heart be troubled, nor let it be fearful.'"

CHAPTER X

Talk to Him

Prayer is a lifeline that leads us to our source of power—Almighty God, Jesus, and the Holy Spirit. One of Jesus' greatest attributes was His prayer life. Scripture is filled with examples of Him praying. All of John 17 is Christ praying. In Luke 22:44, Jesus prays this intensely: "And being in agony He was praying very fervently; and His sweat became like drops of blood, falling down upon the ground."

Jesus started and ended His day talking to His Heavenly Father. Therefore, by His example, it is never out of place for a Christian to pray. It should be like breathing in and breathing out. We are to "pray without ceasing," be "devoted to prayer," and "pray at all times," Paul tells us in I Thessalonians 5:17, Romans 12:12, Colossians 4:2, and Ephesians 6:18.

We should never underestimate the power of prayer or our loving God's desire to hear from us. God is infinite. Let's not insult Him and, in the process, deny ourselves His gifts by making Him anything less. All too often we think we've asked too much or are "bothering" Him with another prayer request. If a friend we adored asked us for something and it was in his best interest to have it, wouldn't we happily accommodate him? We must trust that God not only wants us to bring everything to Him in prayer, but that He will answer our prayers in the way that is most beneficial to us, even if we don't always see it that way.

When we sigh and wearily say, "All we can do now is pray," we are relegating prayer to a last resort when actually it should be our first call to action. Prayer changes things. We *want* to put our concerns and petitions in God's hands. We may not know *what* the future holds, but we can be certain as to *who* holds the future.

God will stay by your side if you stay by His. He hasn't moved. "Evening and morning and at noon, I will complain and murmur, and He will hear my voice....Cast your burden upon the LORD and He will sustain you; He will never allow the righteous to be shaken," Psalm 55:17 and 22 tell us. Leaving God out of our plans is like benching the best player on the team. God is the most effective and important player in the game; He is the go-to guy. He is both the quarterback and the receiver, and we certainly need Him in the huddle.

God has given us the privilege to pray to Him directly, and to address Him confidently and intimately as our "Father."

Consider these Scriptures regarding prayer as well.

- "Come, let us worship and bow down, let us kneel before the LORD our Maker." Psalm 95:6
- "I love the LORD, because He hears my voice *and* my supplications. Because He has inclined His ear to me, therefore I shall call *upon Him* as long as I live." Psalm 116:1-2
- "Then you will call, and the LORD will answer; you will cry, and He will say, `Here I am.'" Isaiah 58:9

- "'Then you will call upon Me and come and pray to Me, and I will listen to you.'" Jeremiah 29:12
- "'Call to Me and I will answer you, and I will tell you great and mighty things, which you do not know.'" Jeremiah 33:3
- "'And all things you ask in prayer, believing, you will receive.'" Matthew 21:22
- "Be anxious for nothing, but in everything by prayer and supplication with thanksgiving let your requests be made known to God." Philippians 4:6
- "Through Him then, let us continually offer up a sacrifice of praise to God, that is, the fruit of lips that give thanks to His name." Hebrews 13:15
- "Is anyone among you suffering? *Then* he must pray. Is anyone cheerful? He is to sing praises." James 5:13
- "...pray for one another so that you may be healed. The effective prayer of a righteous man can accomplish much." James 5:16
- "FOR THE EYES OF THE LORD ARE TOWARD THE RIGHTEOUS, AND HIS EARS ATTEND TO THEIR PRAYER..." I Peter 3:12
- "This is the confidence which we have before Him, that, if we ask anything according to His will, He hears us." I John 5:14

CHAPTER XI

Read the Directions

We might not realize how much we actually appreciate and need rules, definitions, and boundaries in our lives. Despite our desire for independence and individuality, we also crave peace and order, and some rules are vital to that end. Rules of the road, waterways, and air are essential, as are societal rules like waiting our turn in a line, raising our hands in school, and staying seated and quiet in a movie theater. We may say that we don't like rules, but truthfully, we can't and don't want to live without them. We thrive in reasonable order and flounder in chaos.

God's Ten Commandments, which are found in both Exodus 20:3-17 and in Deuteronomy 5:7-21, aren't just a list of rules. Rather, they offer us essential counsel on how we can live happier, healthier, and more productive lives that are pleasing to God, other people, and ourselves.

"'You shall have no other gods before Me. You shall not make for yourself an idol…You shall not take the name of the LORD your God in vain… Observe the sabbath day to keep it holy… Honor your father and your mother… You shall not murder. You shall not commit adultery. You shall not steal. You shall not bear false witness against your neighbor. You shall not covet your neighbor's wife, and you shall not desire your neighbor's house, his field or his male servant or his female servant, his ox or his donkey or anything that belongs to your neighbor.'"

The ramifications of violating some of the commandments, like murder, are obvious. But we need to be more pensive about the dangers disobedience to other commandments may pose. For instance, we may not think that we have any other gods or idols, but we very often do. Our selfishness, vanity, and general self-focus can make us our own gods. Money, careers, popularity, or fame can certainly become idols for many of us. If God isn't first and foremost in our lives, then something else is; our "god" is whatever we think about the most, whatever motivates us the most, and whatever pleases us the most.

Observing the Sabbath is a commandment that most certainly benefits us by encouraging us to worship and have fellowship, both of which boost our spirits and bring us closer to God. Resting on the Sabbath also promotes good health by helping our bodies recuperate from one work week and be ready for another.

The commandment not to bear false witness or lie about someone protects us from scarring, if not ruining, our credibility. Liars need good memories; they have to remember both the lie and the truth, and try to distinguish between them. Lying never has a good outcome. God hates "a lying tongue" and "a false witness *who* utters lies." They are an "abomination to Him," according to Proverbs 6:16, 17 and 19.

The Bible tells us both what not to do and what we ought to do. Jesus sums up the entire biblical system of beliefs and behaviors in these two statements: The greatest and foremost commandment is that we love God with all of our hearts, our souls, and our minds; *and* we must love our neighbors as ourselves. "`On these two commandments depend the whole Law and the Prophets,'" He says in Matthew 22:40.

Jesus did not come to do away with these basic moral principles, but to fulfill them. He is the only one who ever did. Our imperfection makes it impossible for us to fully abide by the Law, but His perfection fully satisfies it. "But now we have been released from the Law, having died to that by which we were bound, so that we serve in newness of the Spirit and not in oldness of the letter." Romans 7:6.

The Old Testament is a covenant between God and man based on laws and regulations. Before we had faith in Jesus Christ, we were held in custody under the Law. The New Testament is a covenant based on love and motivation. As Christians, we should be motivated to follow the Law even though we are no longer controlled by it. "Therefore the Law has become our tutor *to lead us* to Christ, so that we may be justified by faith. But now that faith has come, we are no longer under a tutor." Galatians 3:24-25. In other words, we are not regulated by the Law—which we are incapable of following completely anyway because we are inadequate humans—rather we are freed through Jesus who mastered the Law for us. Despite our guilt, He posted our bail, pled our case, and commuted our prison sentence. "And through Him everyone who believes is freed from all things, from which you could not be freed through the Law of Moses." Acts 13:39.

Galatians 4:4-5 is a beautiful passage of Scripture reminding us of this. It says: "…God sent forth His Son, born of a woman, born under the Law, so that He might redeem those who were under the Law, that we might receive the adoption as sons." Romans 8:16 and 17 describe us as "children of God" and as "heirs of God and fellow heirs with Christ." II Corinthians 6:18 tells us: "'And I will be a father to you, and you shall be sons and daughters to Me,' says the Lord Almighty." We are "all sons of God through faith in Christ Jesus," Galatians 3:26 says.

Being a child of God gives us a perfect parent who has already shown us the ultimate act of love by dying for us, so we can be sure that He wants to help us in every other aspect of our lives. Sin is destructive and chips away at our happiness, our dreams, and our productivity. Each of us is so uniquely important and precious to the Lord; He calls us each by name. King David describes this so poetically in Psalm 139:13-14 (NIV) which says: "For you created my inmost being; you knit me together in my mother's womb. I praise you because I am fearfully and wonderfully made; your works are wonderful, I know that full well." Jesus tells us in Matthew 10:30 and again in Luke 12:7 that God cherishes us so much that He actually knows how many hairs are on each of our heads.

We have a God who totally and completely understands us for who we are as individuals, as well as for who we are as humans in general. "For we do not have a high priest who cannot sympathize with our weaknesses, but One who has been tempted in all things as *we are, yet* without sin." Hebrews 4:15. Jesus' only crime was being perfect in an imperfect world. "For Christ also died for sins once for all, *the* just for *the* unjust, so that He might bring us to God, having been put to death in the flesh, but made alive in the spirit." I Peter 3:18.

These Scriptures tell us how we still must strive to honor the Law, but that Christ fulfills it for us.

- "`Do not think that I came to abolish the Law or the Prophets; I did not come to abolish but to fulfill. For truly I say to you, until heaven and earth pass away, not the smallest letter or stroke shall pass from the Law until all is accomplished.'" Matthew 5:17-18
- "Do we then nullify the Law through faith? May it never be! On the contrary, we establish the Law." Romans 3:31
- "`BLESSED ARE THOSE WHOSE LAWLESS DEEDS HAVE BEEN FORGIVEN, AND WHOSE SINS HAVE BEEN

COVERED. BLESSED IS THE MAN WHOSE SIN THE LORD WILL NOT TAKE INTO ACCOUNT.'" Romans 4:7-8

- "Therefore there is now no condemnation for those who are in Christ Jesus. For the law of the Spirit of life in Christ Jesus has set you free from the law of sin and of death. For what the Law could not do, weak as it was through the flesh, God *did*: sending His own Son in the likeness of sinful flesh and *as an offering* for sin, He condemned sin in the flesh, so that the requirement of the Law might be fulfilled in us, who do not walk according to the flesh but according to the Spirit." Romans 8:1-4
- "For he himself is our peace, who has made the two one and has destroyed the barrier, the dividing wall of hostility, by abolishing in his flesh the law with its commandments and regulations." Ephesians 2:14-15 (NIV)
- "...God made you alive with Christ. He forgave us all our sins, having canceled the written code, with its regulations, that was against us and that stood opposed to us; he took it away, nailing it to the cross." Colossians 2:13-14 (NIV)
- "In fact, the law requires that nearly everything be cleansed with blood, and without the shedding of blood there is no forgiveness." Hebrews 9:22 (NIV)

CHAPTER XII

Not Too Good To Be True

The Bible has been a non-fiction best-seller for hundreds of years. It is the definitive advice book, a history book of the most powerful events and people of all time, and a remarkable book of adventures, like the one Jonah had in the belly of a fish. We should, at the very least, be curious to read it.

We have both internal and external evidence that substantiates the Bible. If we received pieces of broken pottery from forty people from all over the world and found that they fit precisely together to make a perfect vase, we would conclude that they had a common designer. And so it is with the Bible. It contains sixty-six books written over a period of 1,500 years by approximately forty writers, in three languages (Hebrew, Greek, and Aramaic), on three continents (Asia, Africa, and Europe), and yet is a perfect unit from cover to cover. We must conclude that it has a common designer—Almighty God! What a wonderful book!

For many years, the oldest copy of the complete Hebrew Old Testament was the Leningrad Codex or Manuscript, dated at about 1000 A.D. Critics claimed that it was hopelessly corrupted because it had been copied often from the original Old Testament, which was completed in approximately 400 B.C., to its writing 1,400 years later.

Remarkably, an almost complete manuscript of Isaiah was found in 1947 as part of the archeological find called the Dead Sea Scrolls. The Isaiah scrolls were dated to at least 100 B.C., nearly 1,100 years earlier than the Leningrad Manuscript. Yet, when the two documents were compared, they matched in each minute detail. The Leningrad Codex was not sullied, rather it was validated, and it corroborated the much earlier text of the Dead Sea Scrolls.

The Old Testament starts with Moses' writing of the first five books of the Bible in approximately 1450 B.C., and ends with the prophet Malachi's book, which he wrote about 1,000 years later. The New Testament starts with the four Gospels—Matthew, Mark, Luke, and John. The Gospel writers' descriptions of Jesus' birth, teachings, crucifixion, and resurrection were written about 65 years after Jesus' death and more than 500 years after Malachi's book. Despite the long gap between the Old and New Testament writings, they are completely interwoven and essential to one another.

The Old Testament is the New Testament concealed. The New Testament is the Old Testament revealed. Together they are perfect and complete. For instance, there are more than 300 fulfilled prophecies about Jesus in the Old Testament. All of Isaiah 53 is an astoundingly detailed foretelling of Christ's mission, yet it was written about 700 years before He was even born. Isaiah's prophetic descriptions of Jesus include: "He was despised and forsaken of men" (verse 3); "the LORD has caused the iniquity of us all to fall on Him" (verse 6); "He would render Himself *as* a guilt offering" (verse 10); and "He Himself bore the sin of many, and interceded for the transgressors" (verse 12). Consider these excerpts from verses 3 and 4: "He was despised, and we did not esteem

Him. Surely our griefs He Himself bore, and our sorrows He carried." Verse 5 continues: "But He was pierced through for our transgressions, He was crushed for our iniquities; the chastening for our well-being *fell* upon Him, and by His scourging we are healed."

Jesus acknowledges that He is the fulfillment of these prophecies *before* His arrest and crucifixion when He says: "`Now My soul has become troubled; and what shall I say, `Father, save Me from this hour'? But for this purpose I came to this hour.'" John 12:27. "`...All things which are written through the prophets about the Son of Man will be accomplished,'" He says in Luke 18:31. While being arrested, Jesus says, "`But all this has taken place to fulfill the Scriptures of the prophets.'" Matthew 26:56 and Mark 14:49.

After His resurrection, Jesus reminds His followers: "`These are My words which I spoke to you while I was still with you, that all things which are written about me in the Law of Moses and the Prophets and the Psalms must be fulfilled.'" Luke 24:44. Jesus is also described as "this *Man*, delivered over by the predetermined plan and foreknowledge of God" in Acts 2:23.

Isaiah also tells us about Christ's birth. "For a child will be born to us, a son will be given to us; and the government will rest on His shoulders; and His name will be called Wonderful Counselor, Mighty God, Eternal Father, Prince of Peace." Isaiah 9:6. "`Therefore the Lord Himself will give you a sign: Behold, a virgin will be with child and bear a son, and she will call His name Immanuel.'" Isaiah 7:14. This divine foretelling was most surely realized, as Matthew 1:20-25 tells us. An angel of the Lord appears to Joseph in a dream and tells him, "`She will bear a Son; and you shall call His name Jesus, for He will save His people from their sins.'"

The pre-existence of the unborn Christ is also confirmed in I Peter 1:20-21, which says: "For He was foreknown before the foundation of the world, but has appeared in these last times for the sake of you who through Him are believers in God…" John describes Christ as "Him who has been from the beginning" in both I John 2:13 and 14. Jesus also refers to His pre-existence in John 17:24 and in John 17:5 (NCV) when He says in prayer, "'And now, Father, give me glory with you; give me the glory I had with you before the world was made.'"

Both the birth of Christ in a rather obscure little town in Judea called Bethlehem and His lineage through David, whose father was Jesse, is also prophesied in the Old Testament. God tells us this in Micah 5:2: "'But as for you, Bethlehem Ephrathah, *too* little to be among the clans of Judah, from you One will go forth for Me to be ruler in Israel.'" Another very specific prophecy can be found in Isaiah 11:1-2: "Then a shoot will spring from the stem of Jesse, and a branch from his roots will bear fruit. The Spirit of the LORD will rest on Him…"

That fulfillment in the New Testament reads: "Joseph also went up from Galilee, from the city of Nazareth, to Judea, to the city of David which is called Bethlehem, because he was of the house and family of David, in order to register along with Mary, who was engaged to him, and was with child. While they were there, the days were completed for her to give birth. And she gave birth to her firstborn son…" Luke 2:4-7.

The Old Testament also gives a more vivid picture of the crucifixion than is found in the Gospels. "A band of evildoers has encompassed me; they pierced my hands and my feet. I can count all my bones. They look, they stare at me; they divide my garments among them, and for my clothing they cast lots." Psalm 22:16-18.

The Old Testament prophesizes: "A band of evildoers has encompassed me." The New Testament fulfills: "Then the soldiers of the governor took Jesus into the Praetorium and gathered the whole *Roman* cohort around Him." Matthew 27:27.

The Old Testament prophesizes: “They look, they stare at me.” The New Testament fulfills: Golgotha, the place where Jesus was crucified, was near the city of Jerusalem. Chief priests, scribes, elders, centurions, soldiers, bystanders, and Jesus’ supporters comprised what Luke 23:4 and 48 describe as “the crowds” or “the multitudes.” Many people witnessed His sentencing and crucifixion, and read the sign that Pontius Pilate (the Roman governor who ordered Jesus’ crucifixion) installed on the cross: “JESUS THE NAZARENE, THE KING OF THE JEWS,” which was written in Hebrew, Latin, and Greek. John 19:19-20.

It is historically significant that Jesus’ death on the cross was well-witnessed by both believers and non-believers. There is absolutely no question that Jesus did die on that cross. It’s what happened after that, also documented and witnessed by many, that changed the world forever. Matthew 27:57-66 tells us that Pilate allowed a man named Joseph from Arimathea to take Jesus’ body, which he then placed in a tomb he had carved out of a rock. Joseph then closed off the only entrance to the cave-like tomb with a large stone. But Pilate, the chief priests, and the Pharisees were concerned that Jesus’ disciples would hide His body to convince non-believers that He had risen from the dead. Therefore, they made sure that the tomb was secured, sealed, and well guarded.

It was no barrier, however, for the angel of the Lord who came and rolled away the stone. Thc angel’s “appearance was like lightning, and his clothing as white as snow. The guards shook for fear of him and became like dead men.” Matthew 28:3-4. The angel did not roll the stone away to let Jesus out of His tomb. Rather, the tomb was unblocked to allow witnesses in to see a corpse-less grave. Both followers and enemies alike were looking for His body, not the living Christ.

If Jesus’ enemies could have produced a dead body, there would be no Christianity today. Jesus’ resurrection confirmed both the message and the messenger. This is the greatest historical fact of all time. "'This Jesus God raised up again, to which we are all witnesses,'" Peter confirms in Acts 2:32. Paul tells us in I Corinthians 15:6 that the resurrected Christ not only appeared to His disciples, but that "more than five hundred brethren at one time" witnessed Him alive after He was dead and buried.

The Old Testament prophesizes: "They pierced my hands and my feet. I can count all my bones" in Psalm 22:16-17 and "'they will look on Me whom they have pierced'" in Zechariah 12:10. The New Testament fulfills: Gospel writer John, who was an eyewitness to Jesus' crucifixion, describes the nail wounds in Jesus' hands and His pierced side in John 20:25 and 27. John further describes Jesus' bones being intact and counted, as foretold in Psalms, by describing how the Jews asked Pilate to have the legs of Jesus and the men crucified alongside Him broken to hasten their deaths so that their bodies could be removed before the Sabbath. "So the soldiers came, and broke the legs of the first man and of the other who was crucified with Him; but coming to Jesus, when they saw that He was already dead, they did not break His legs. But one of the soldiers pierced His side with a spear, and immediately blood and water came out." John 19:32-34.

The Old Testament prophesizes: "They divide my garments among them, and for my clothing they cast lots." The New Testament fulfills: All four Gospel writers confirm the disbursement of Jesus' clothing as described in Psalms. Those accounts can be found in Matthew 27:35, Mark 15:24, Luke 23:34, and John 19:23-24, which says: "Then the soldiers, when they had crucified Jesus, took His outer garments and made four parts, a part to every soldier and *also* the tunic; now the tunic was seamless, woven in one piece. So they said to one another, 'Let us not tear it, but cast lots for it, *to decide* whose it shall be...'"

It is a horrible image, yet one that was foretold and realized. Did the men gambling for Jesus' meager clothing ever come to know who He really was? Did they eventually turn to the Scriptures and embrace the man whose clothes they had once hoped to win? Did they learn to stand firm and in the peace of the Gospel? Did they learn to use God's armor—the belt of truth, the breastplate of righteousness, the shoes of peace, the shield of faith, the helmet of salvation, and the sword of the Spirit, which is the word of God—as described in Ephesians 6:14-17?

We can only wonder what their fate may have been, but let us not take a chance ourselves by not being prepared. Let us be sure to recognize God the Father, the Son, and the Holy Spirit by being well-read in the Scriptures, and thus stand firmly and knowledgably in our faith. Our goal should be to emulate the people Paul describes in Acts 17:11 who "received the word with great eagerness, examining the Scriptures daily *to see* whether these things were so." In fact, the Bible does tell us so. Rejoice!